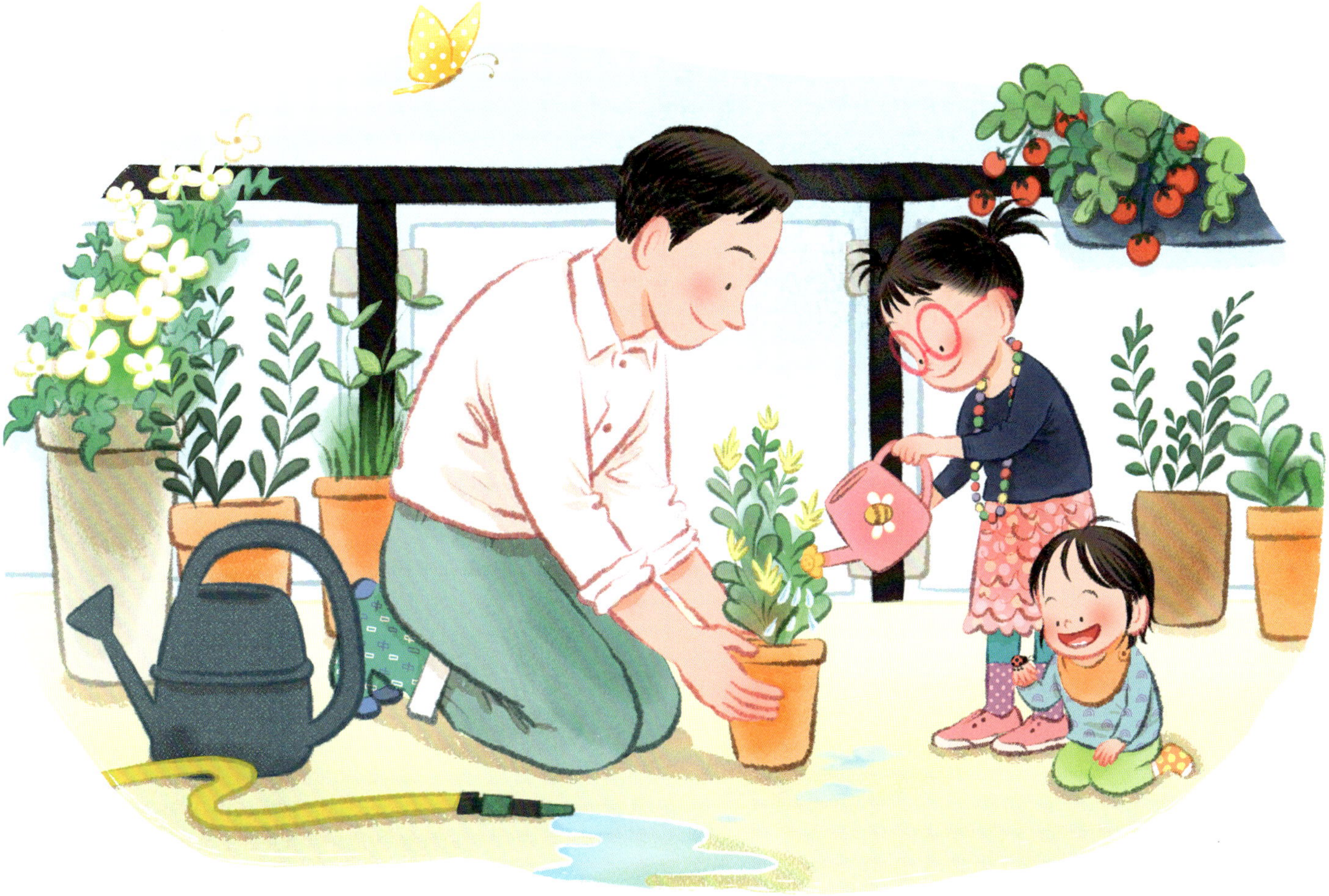

A big day in

Sungsu Heaven

Collins

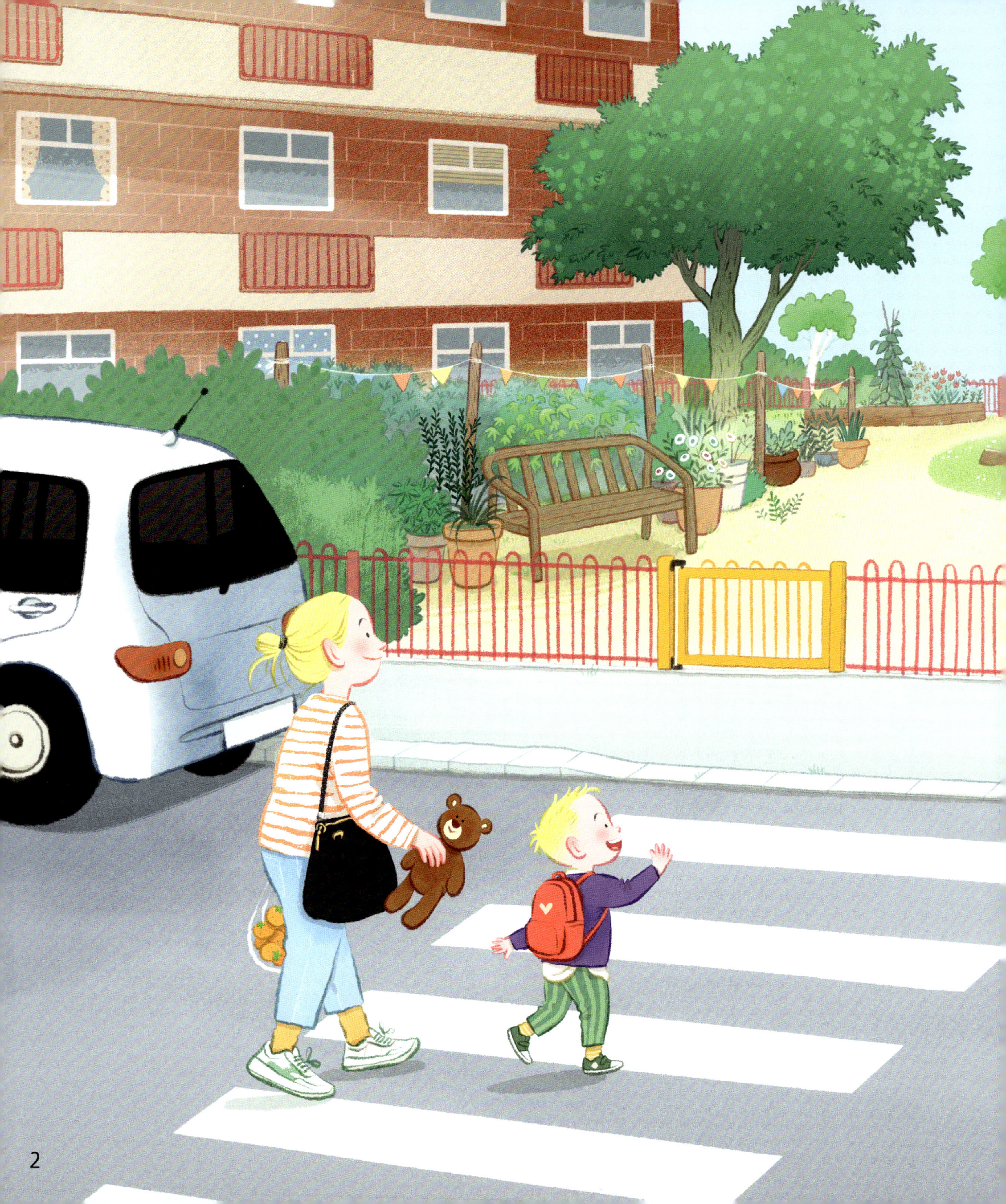

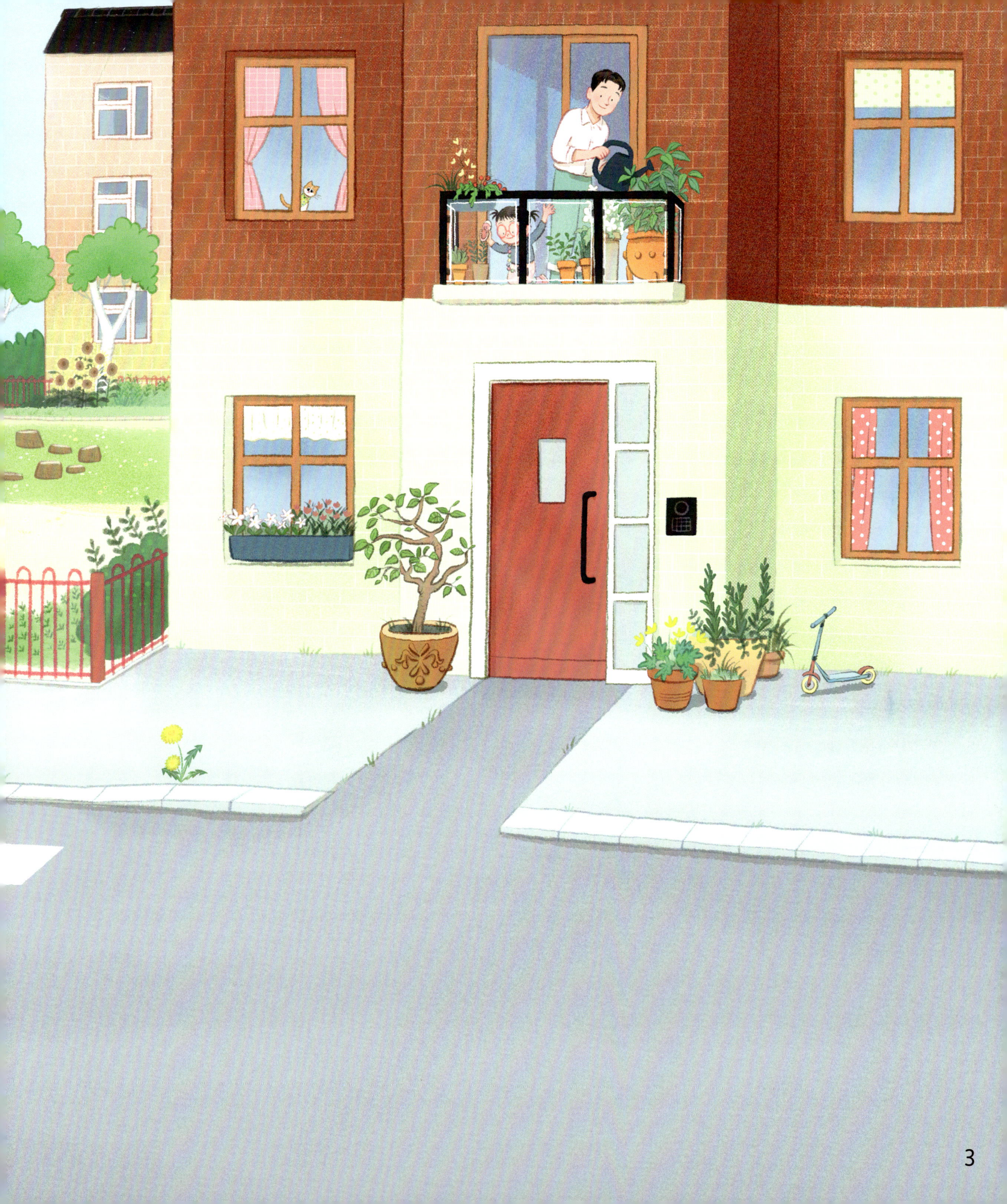

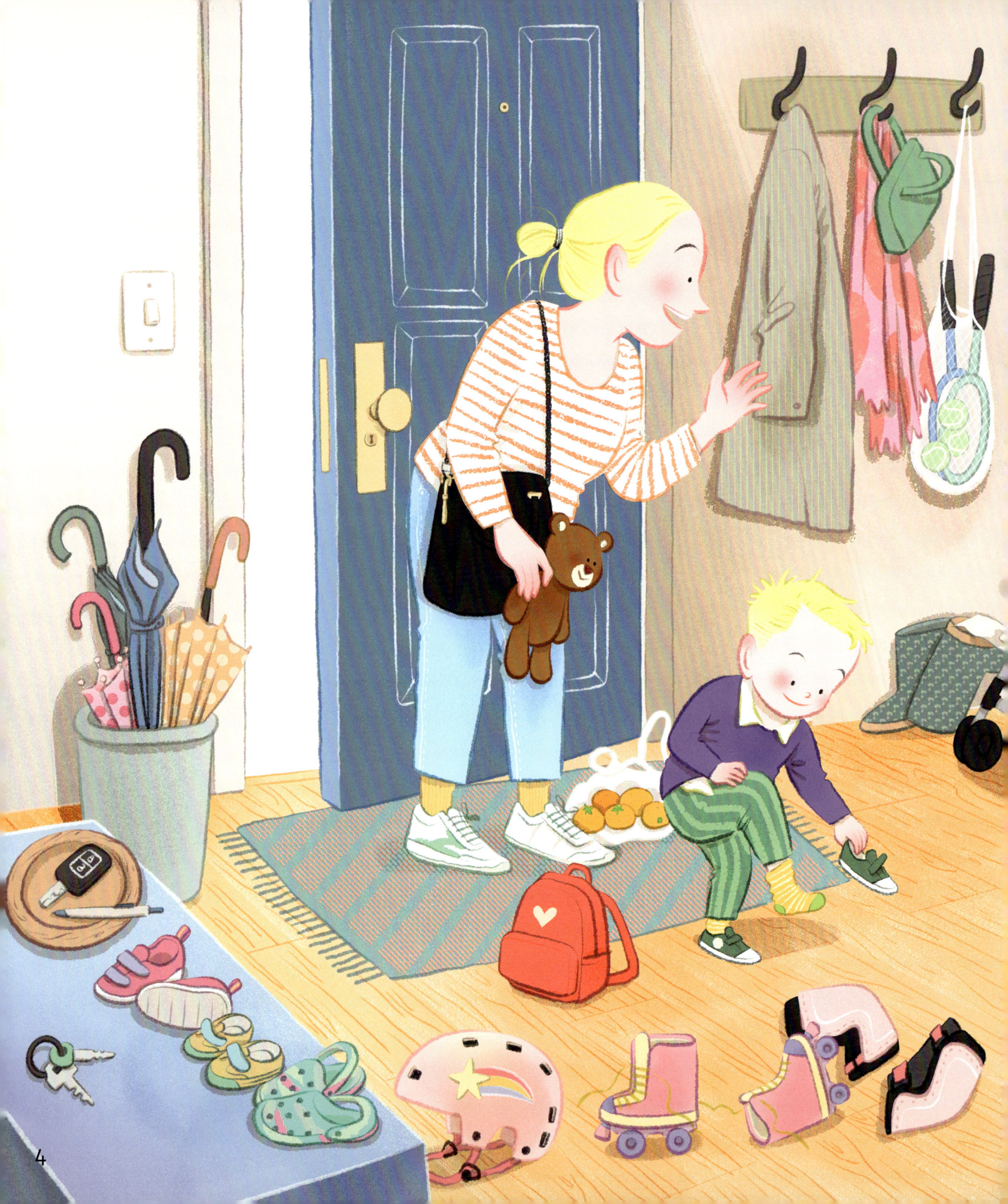

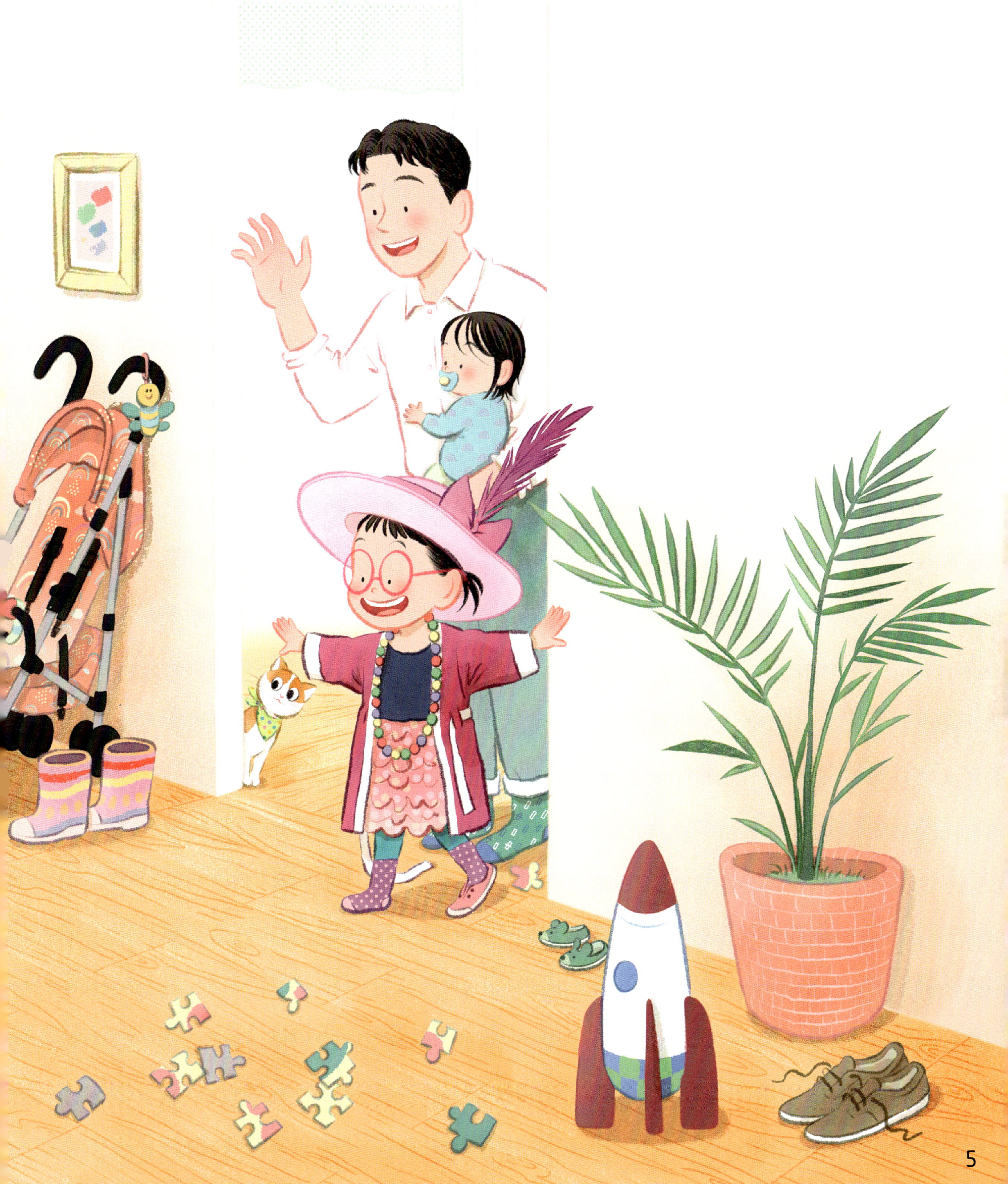

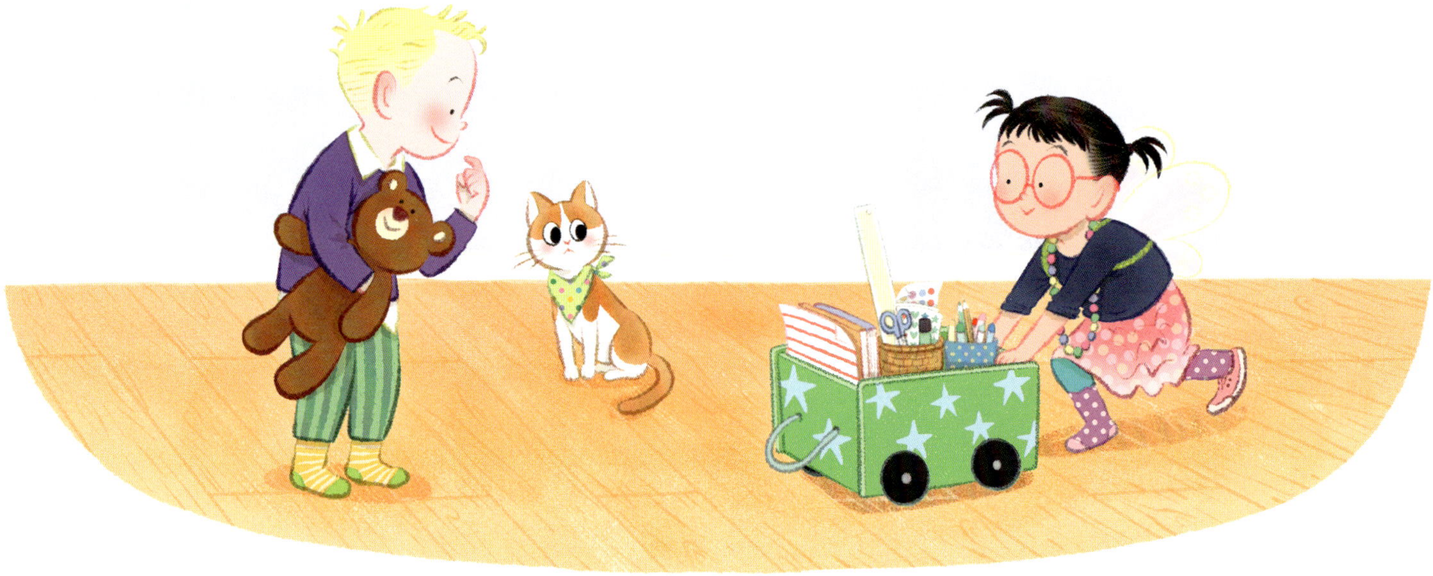

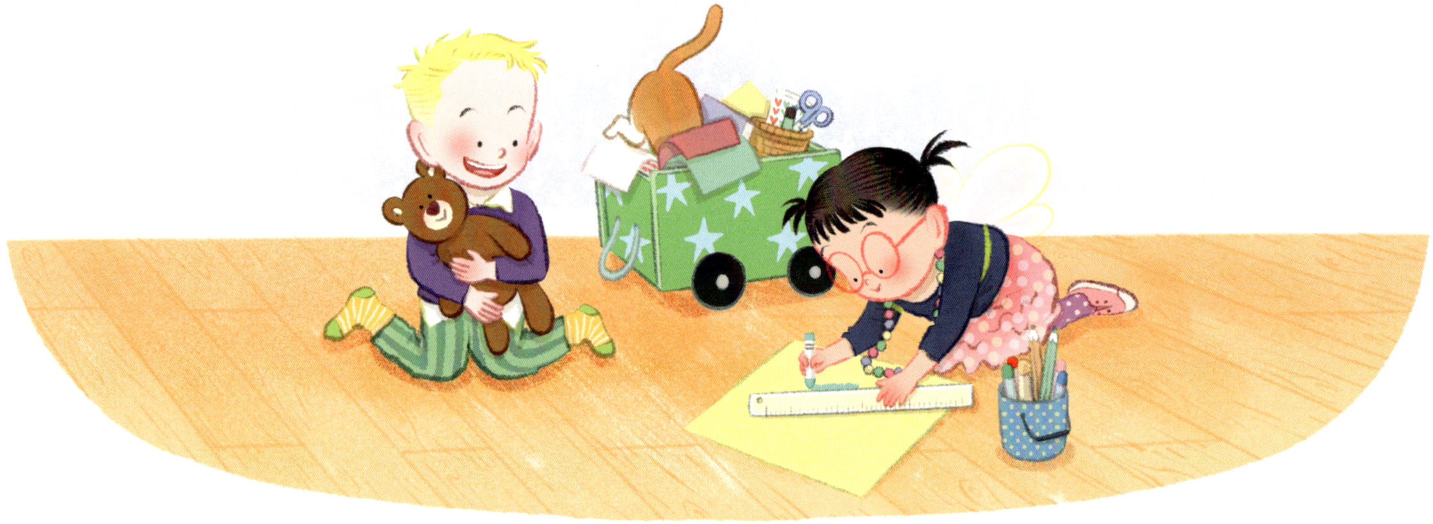

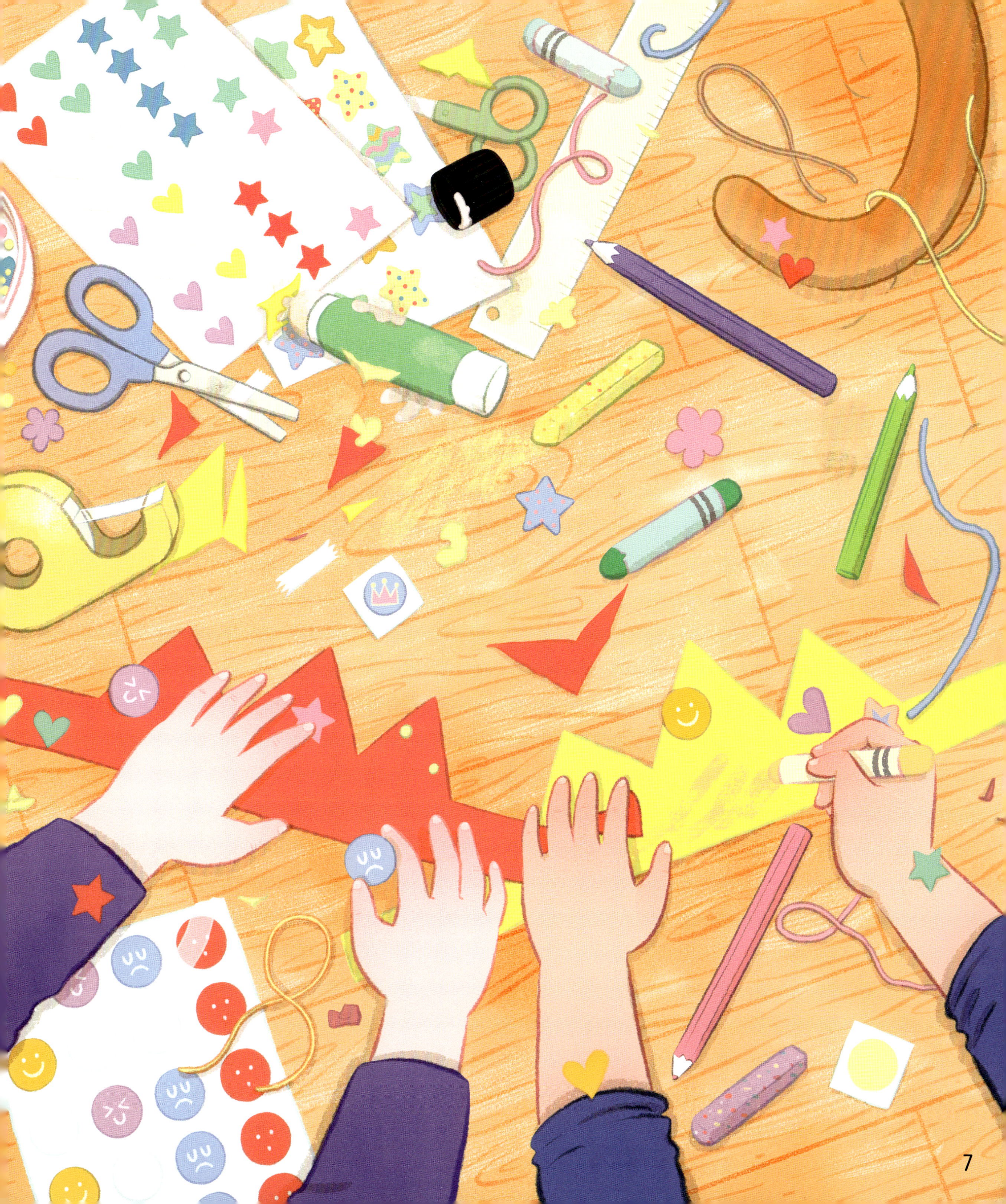

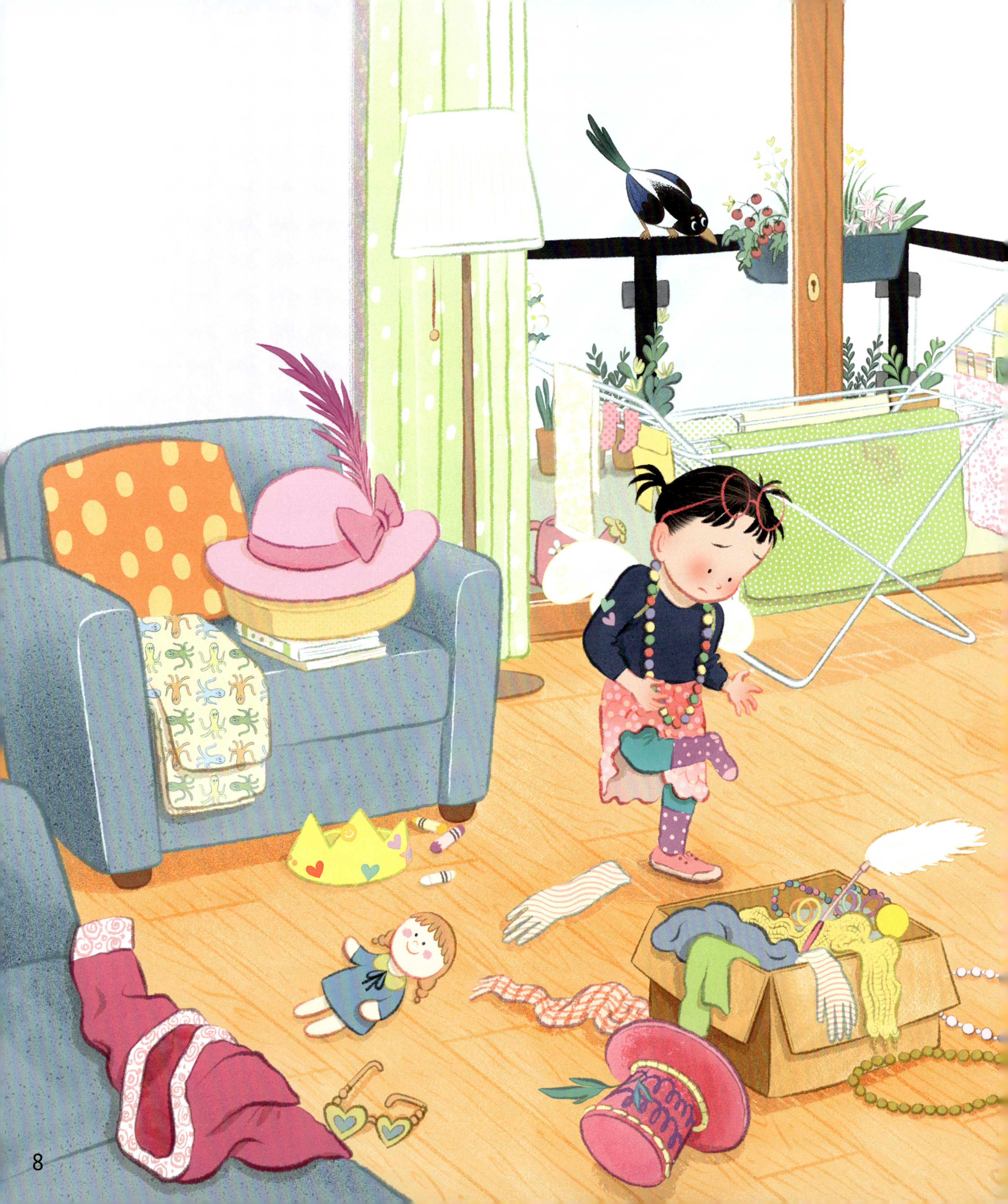

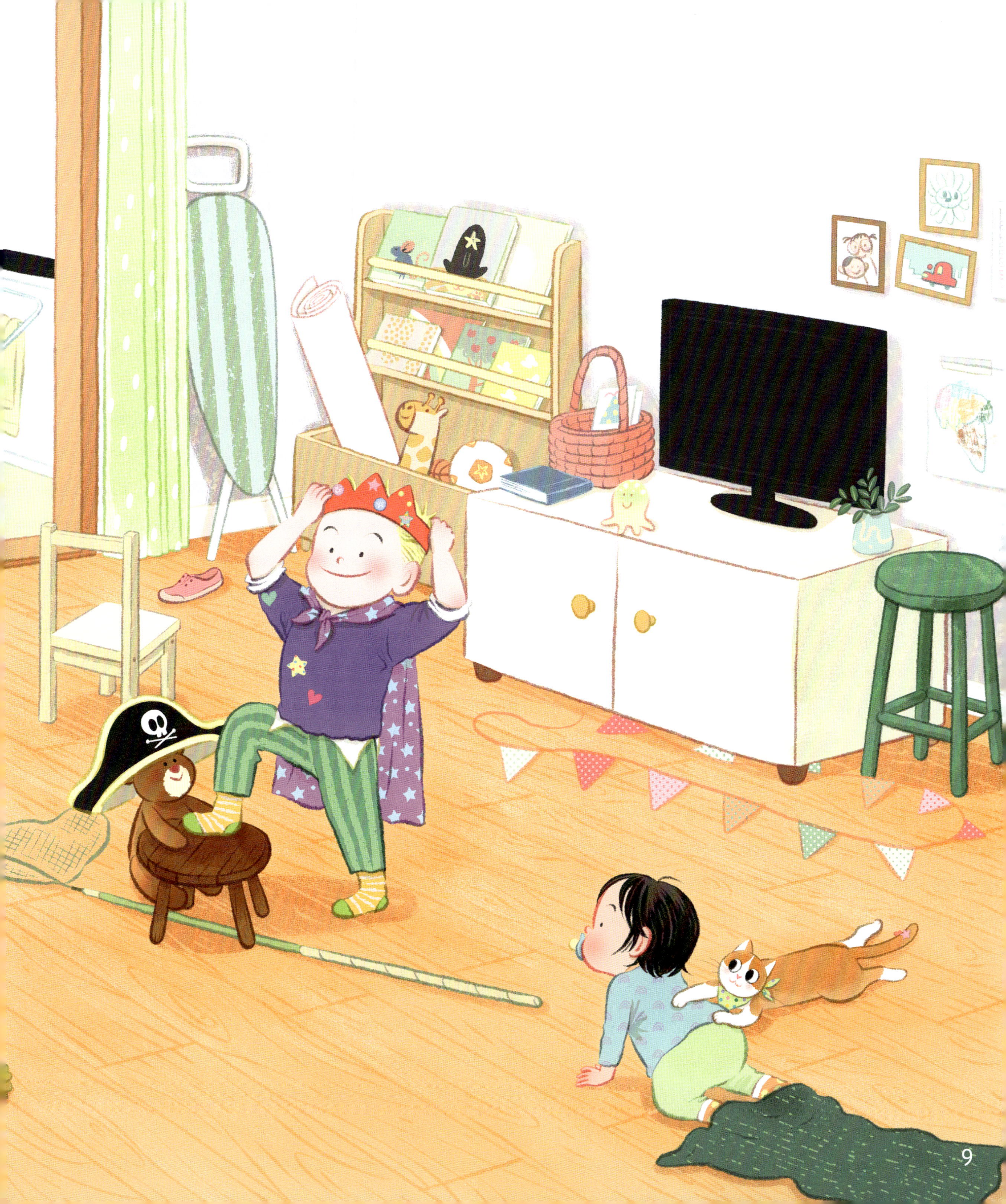

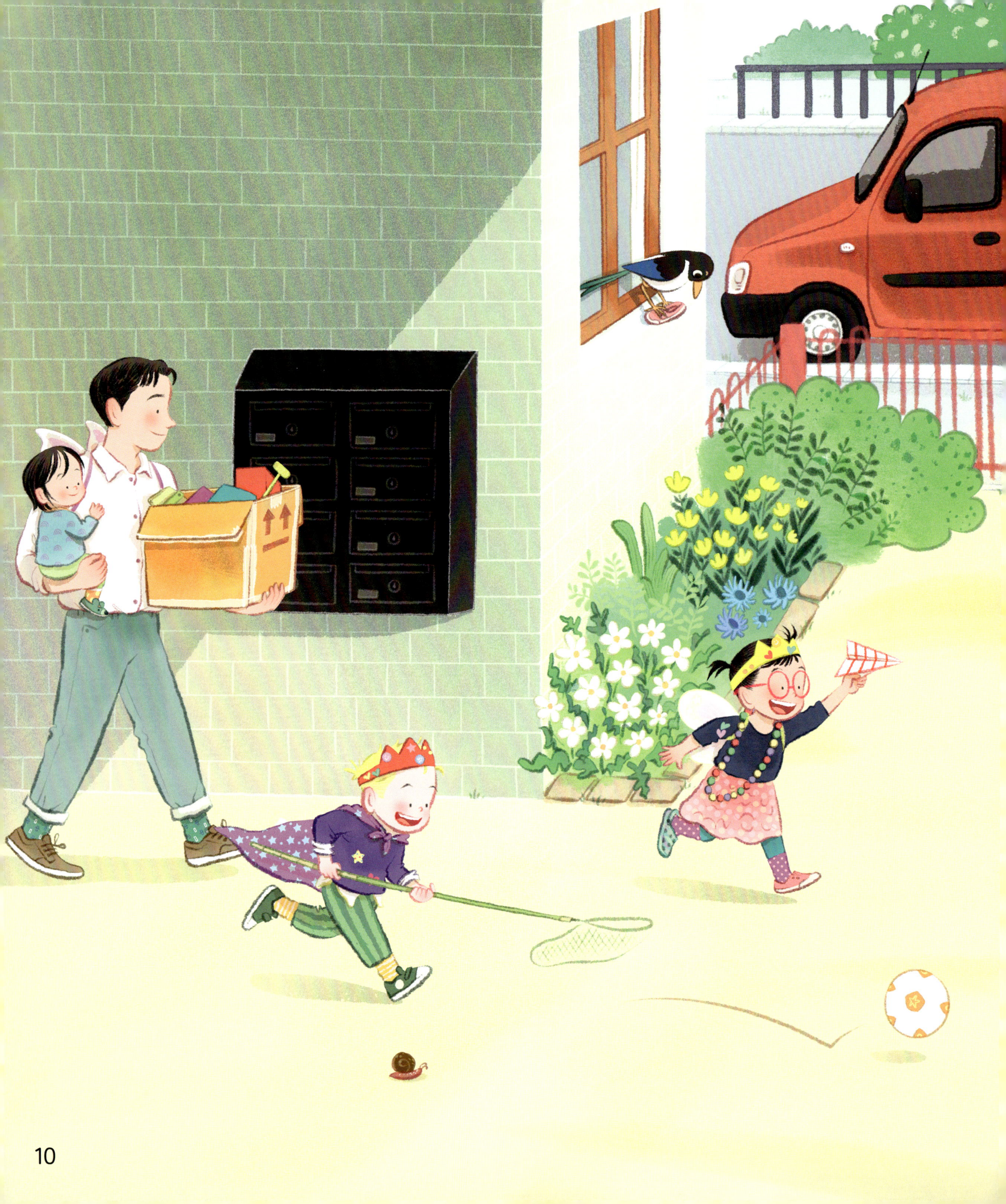

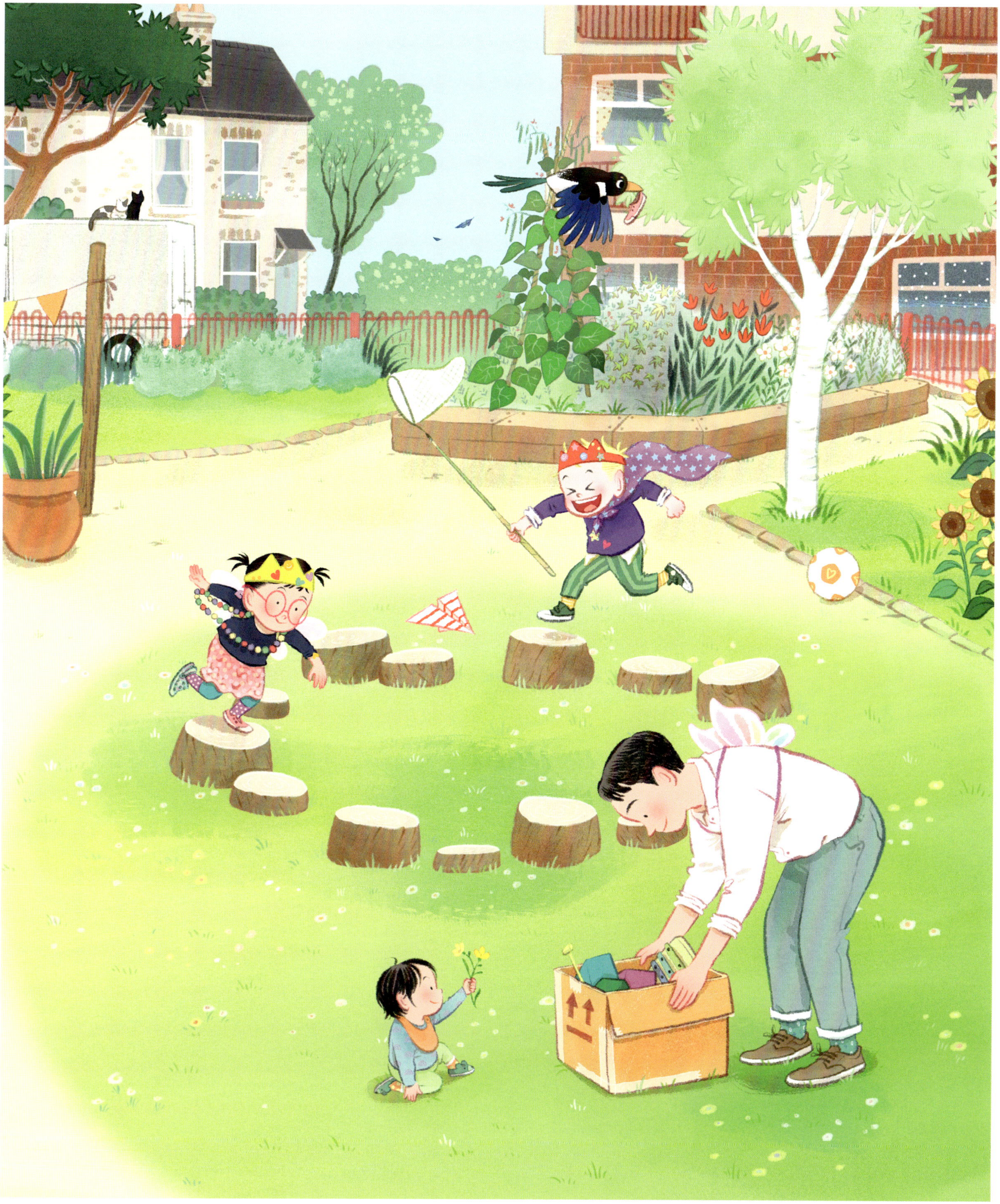

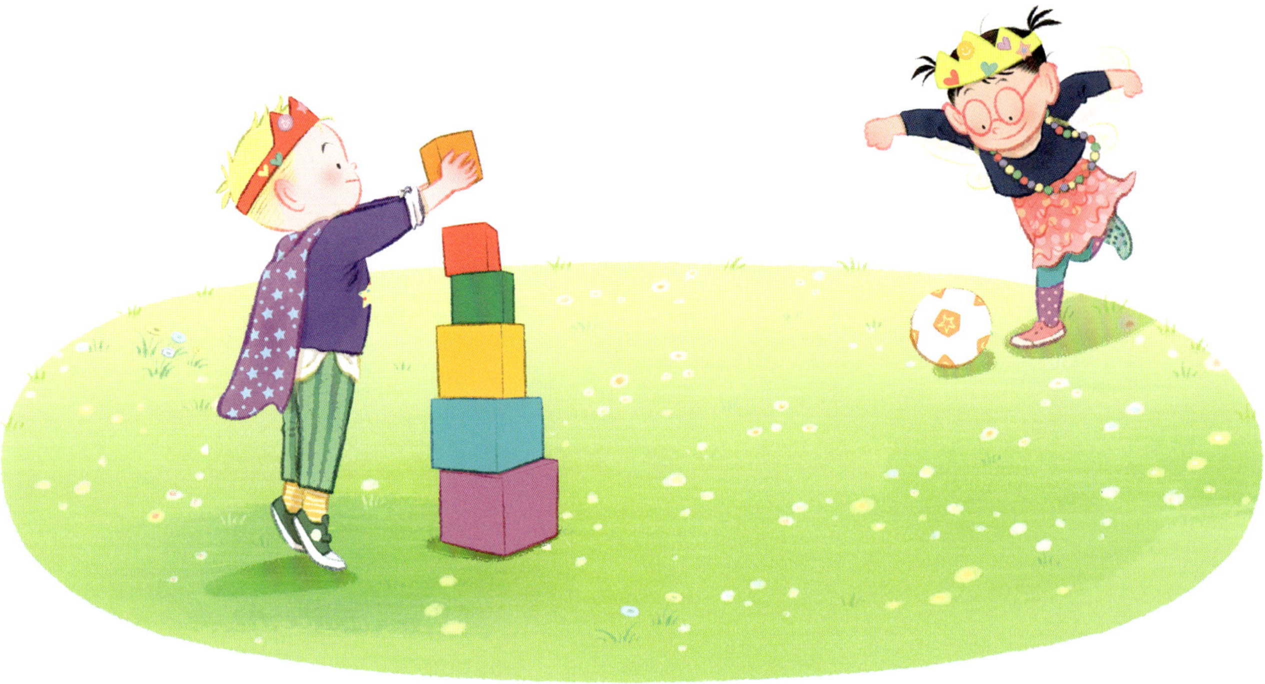

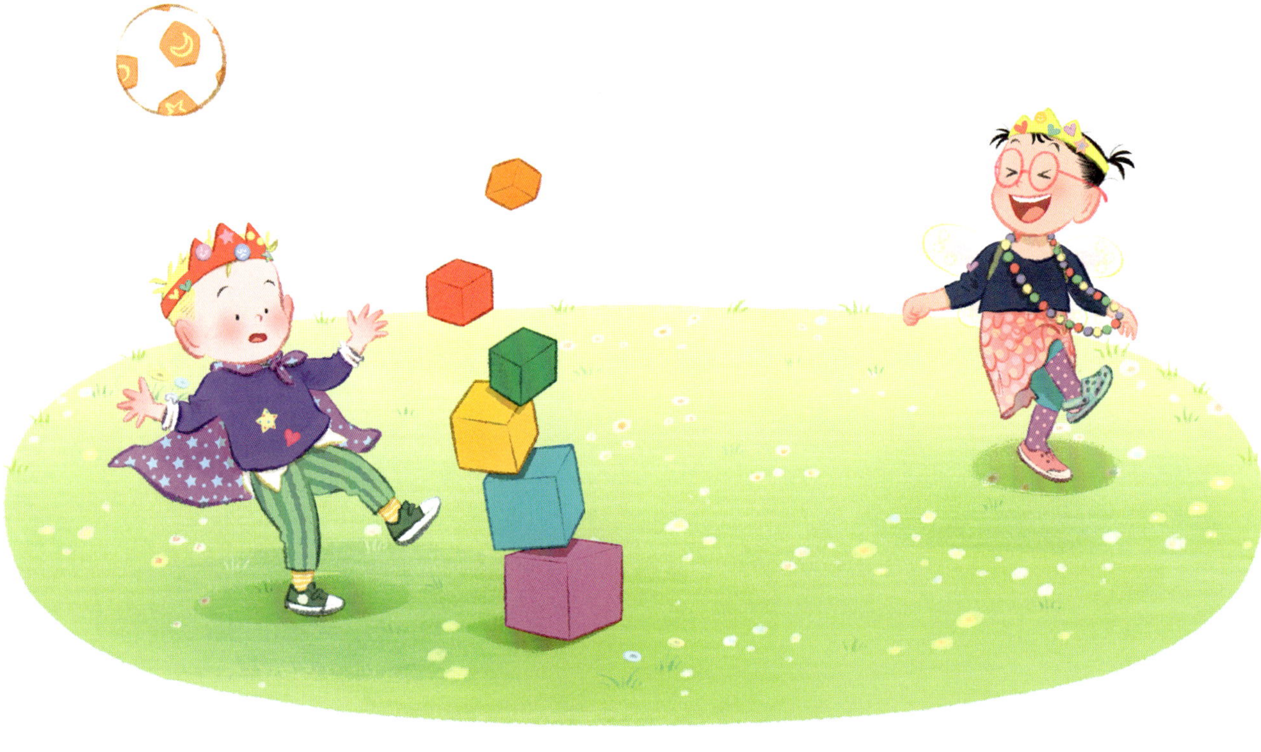

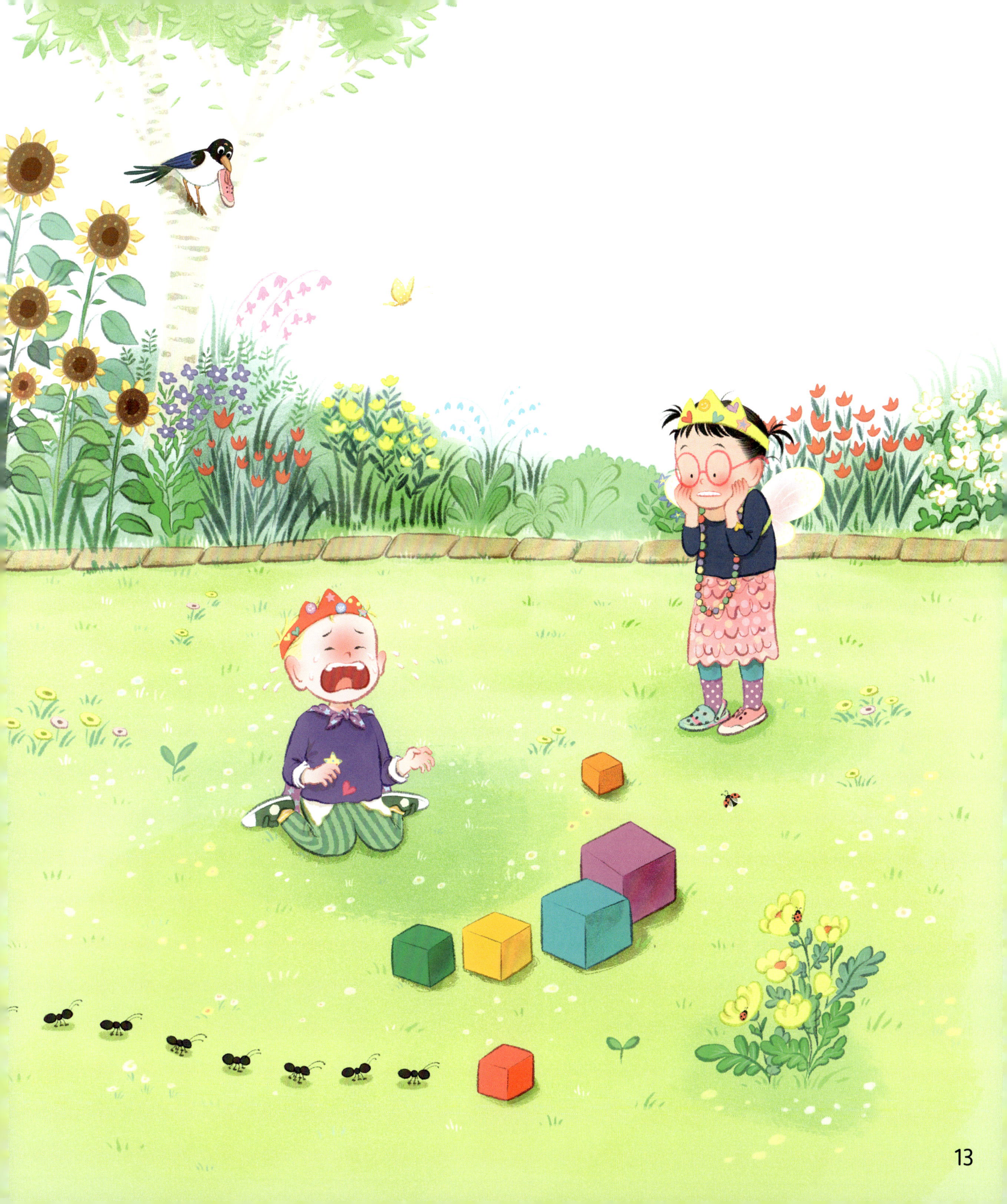

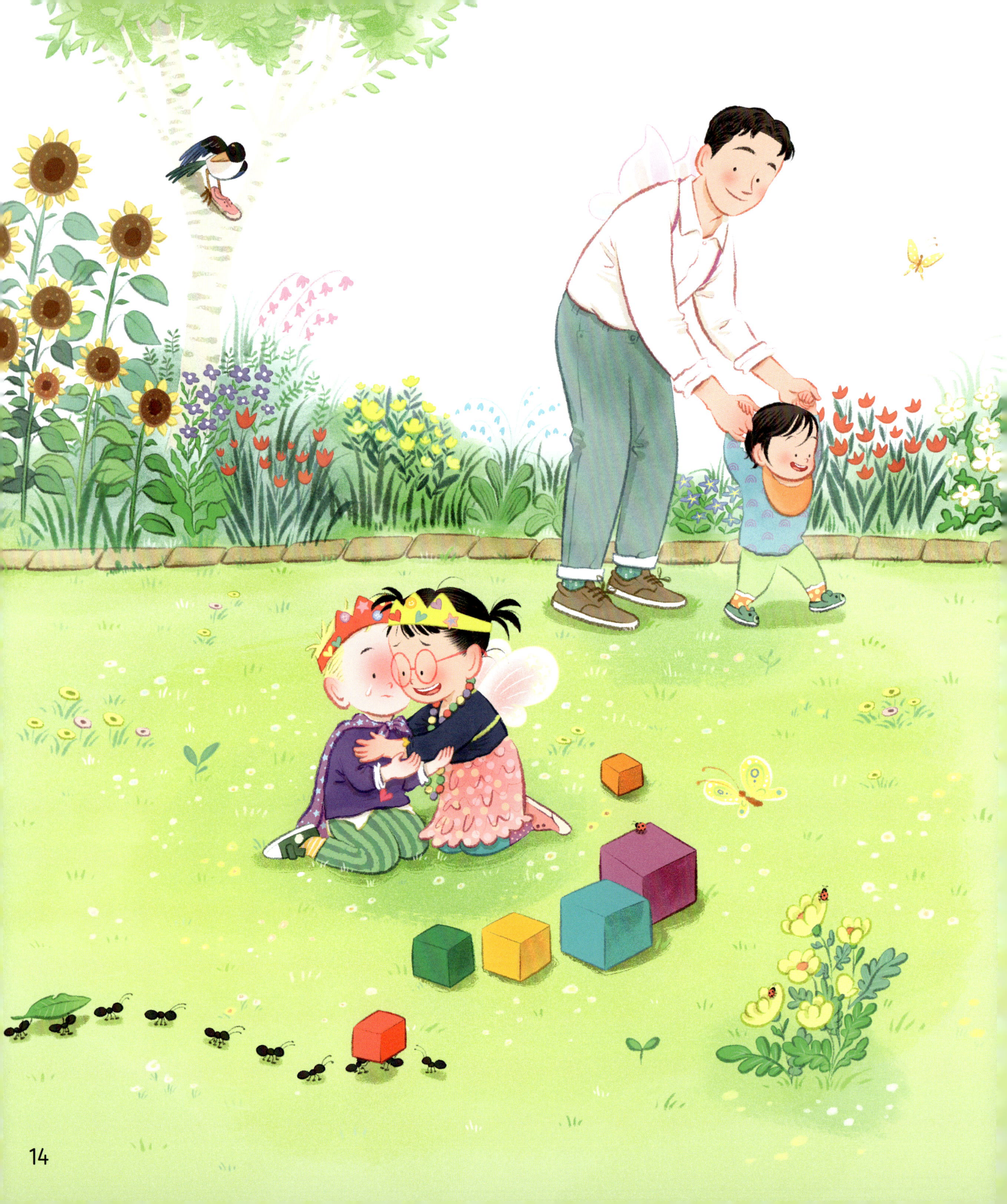

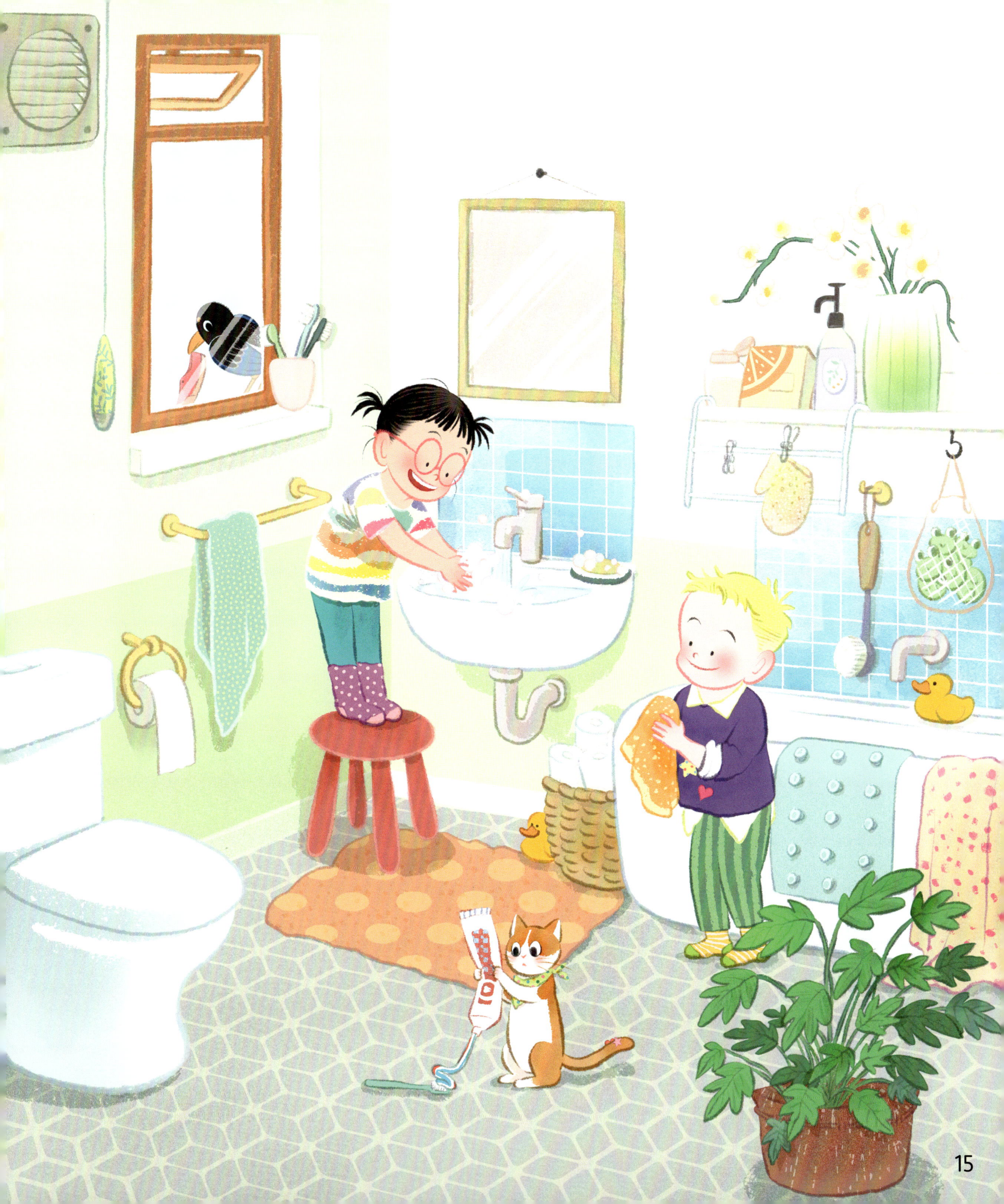

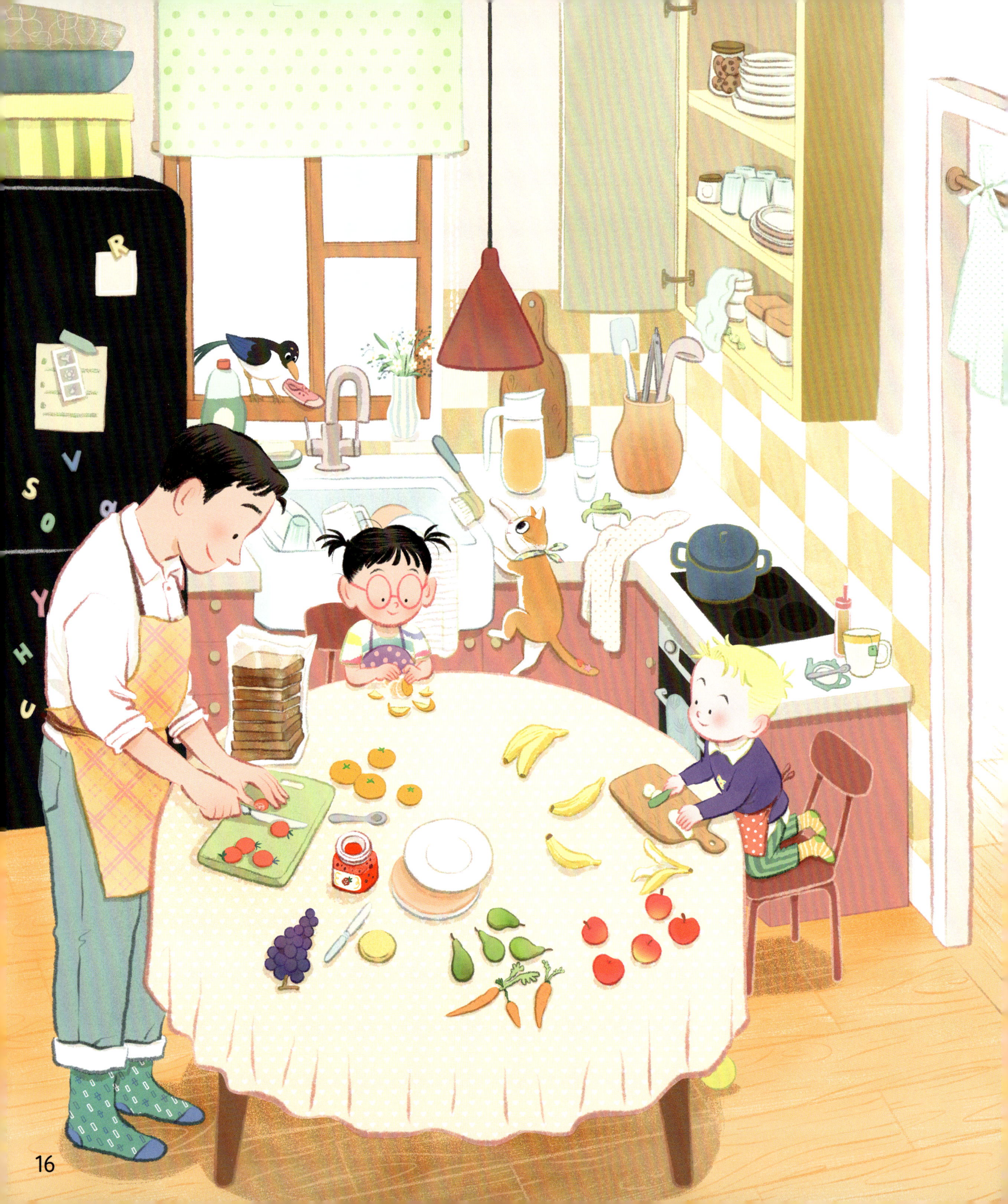

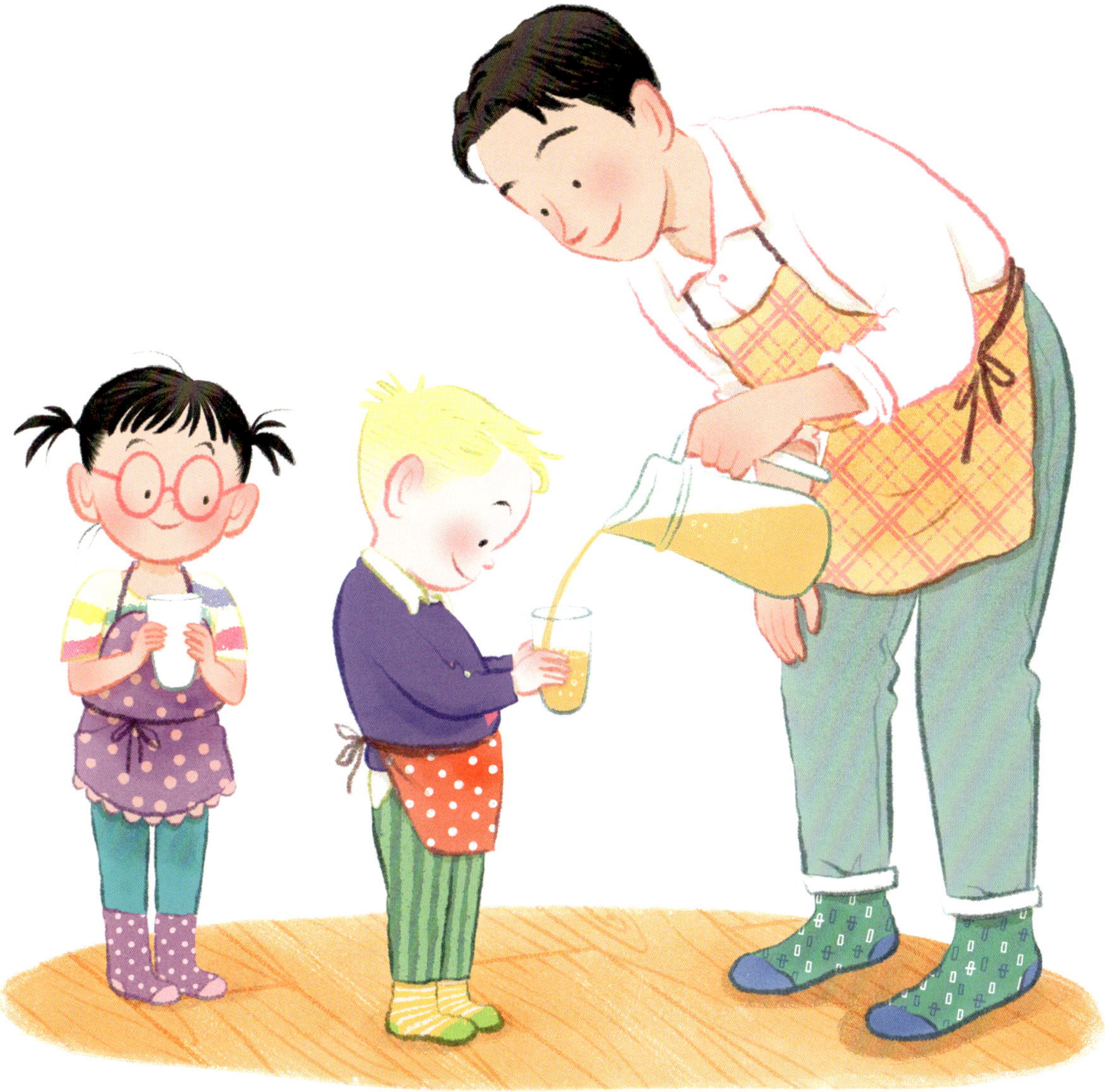

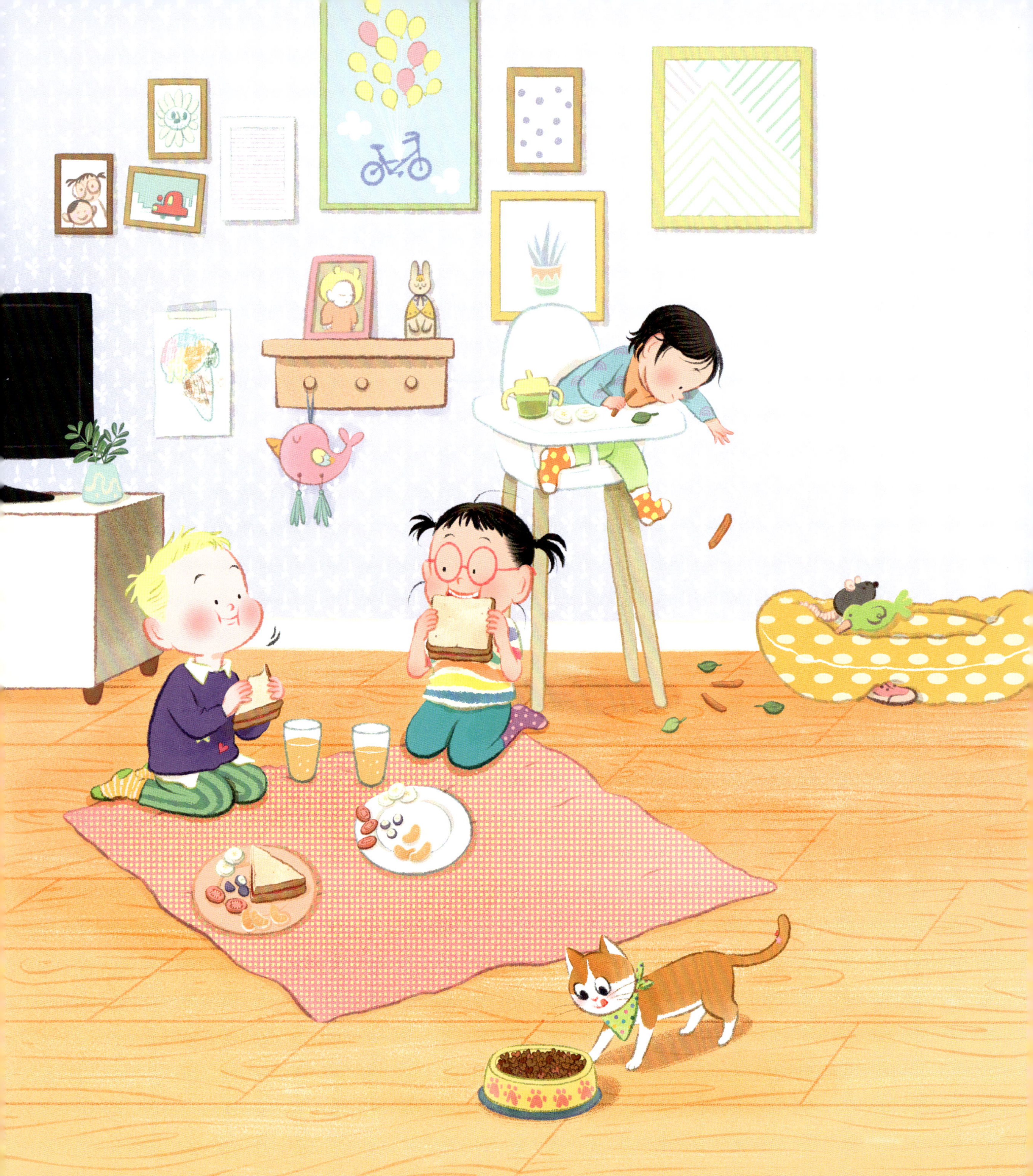

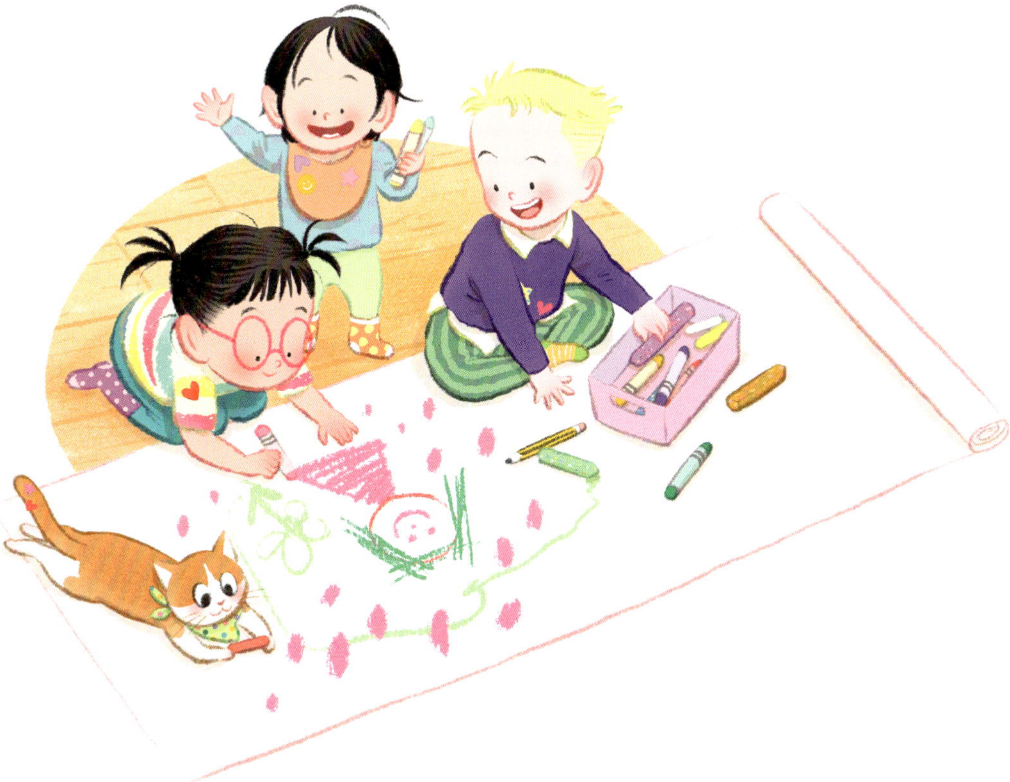

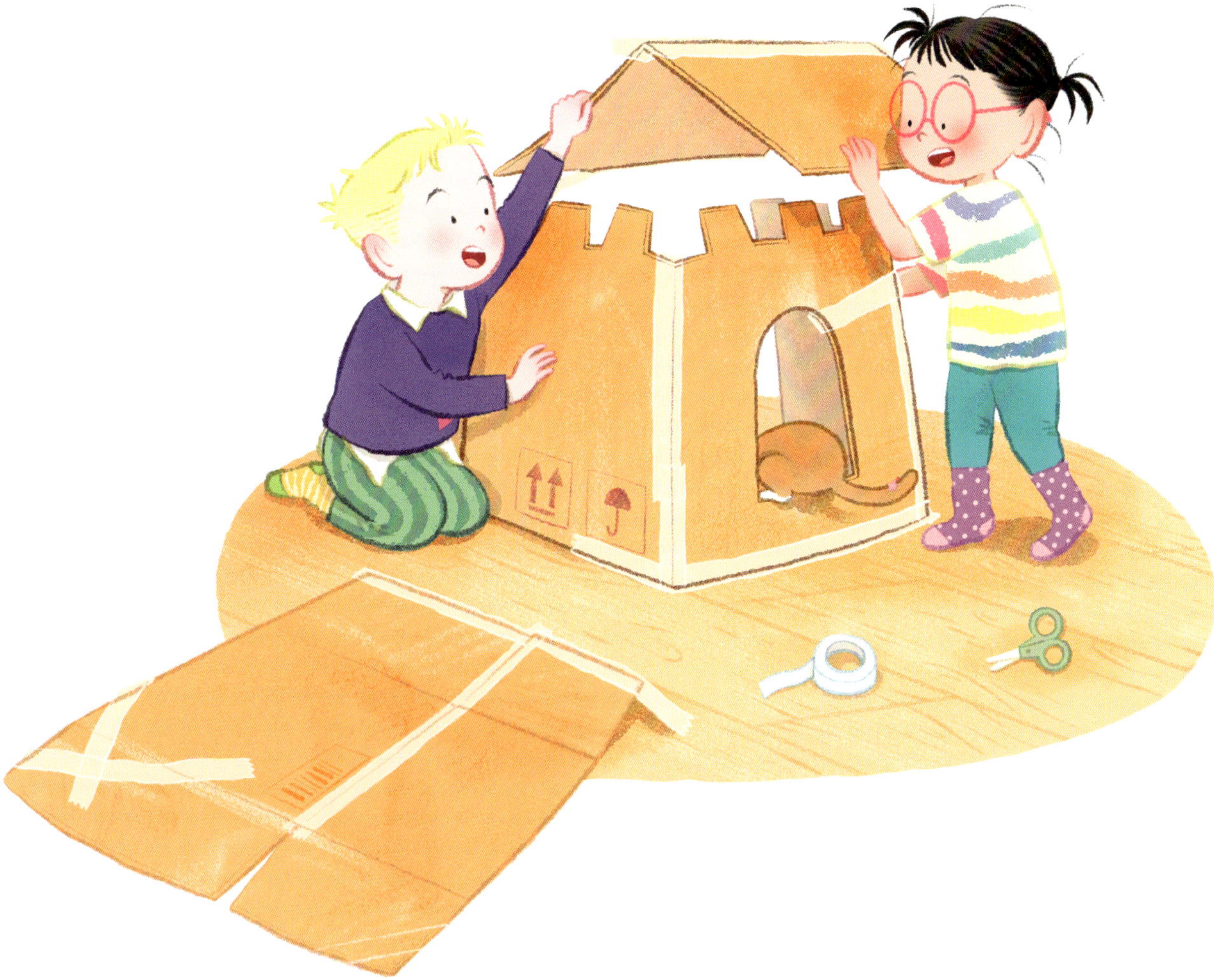

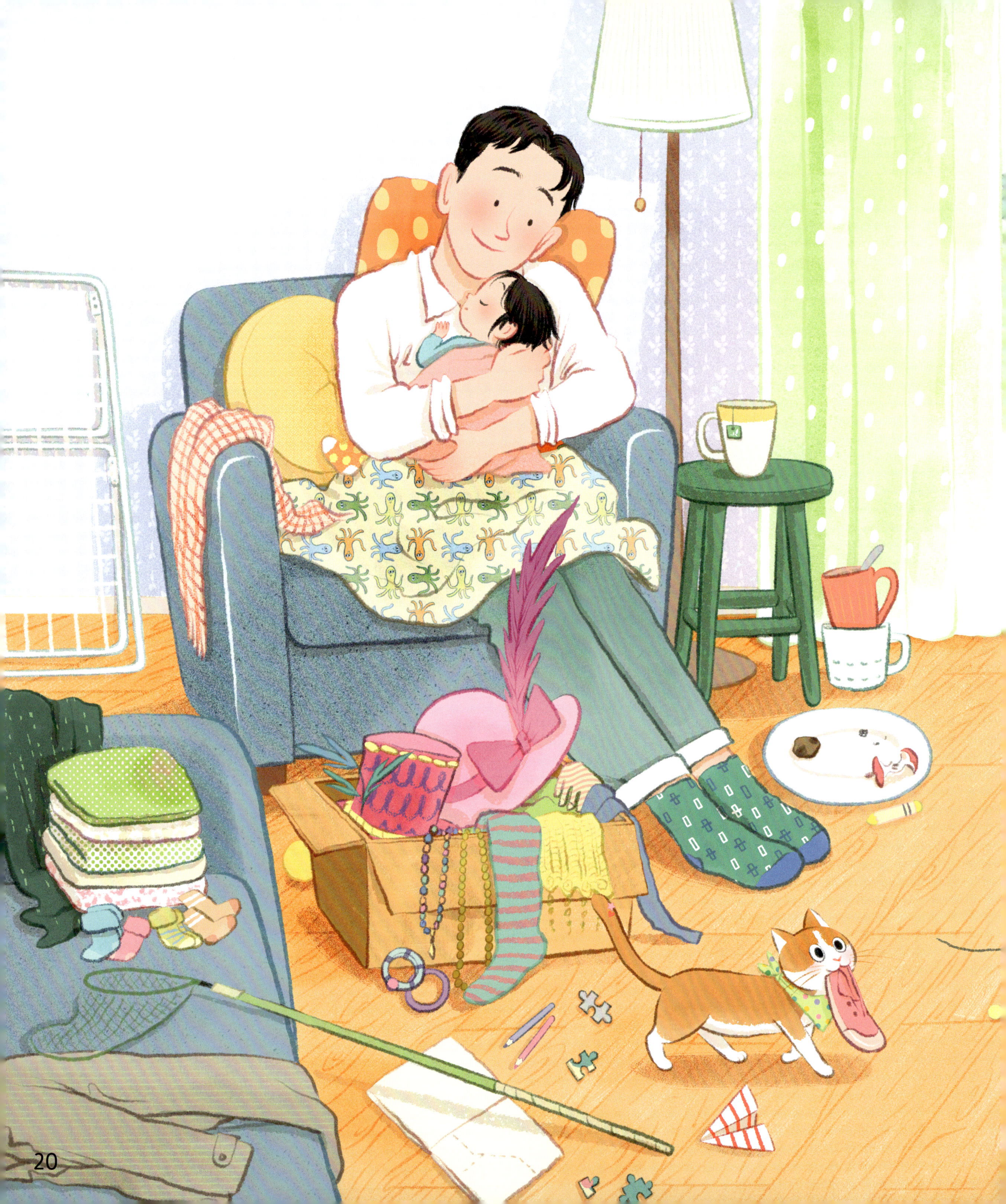

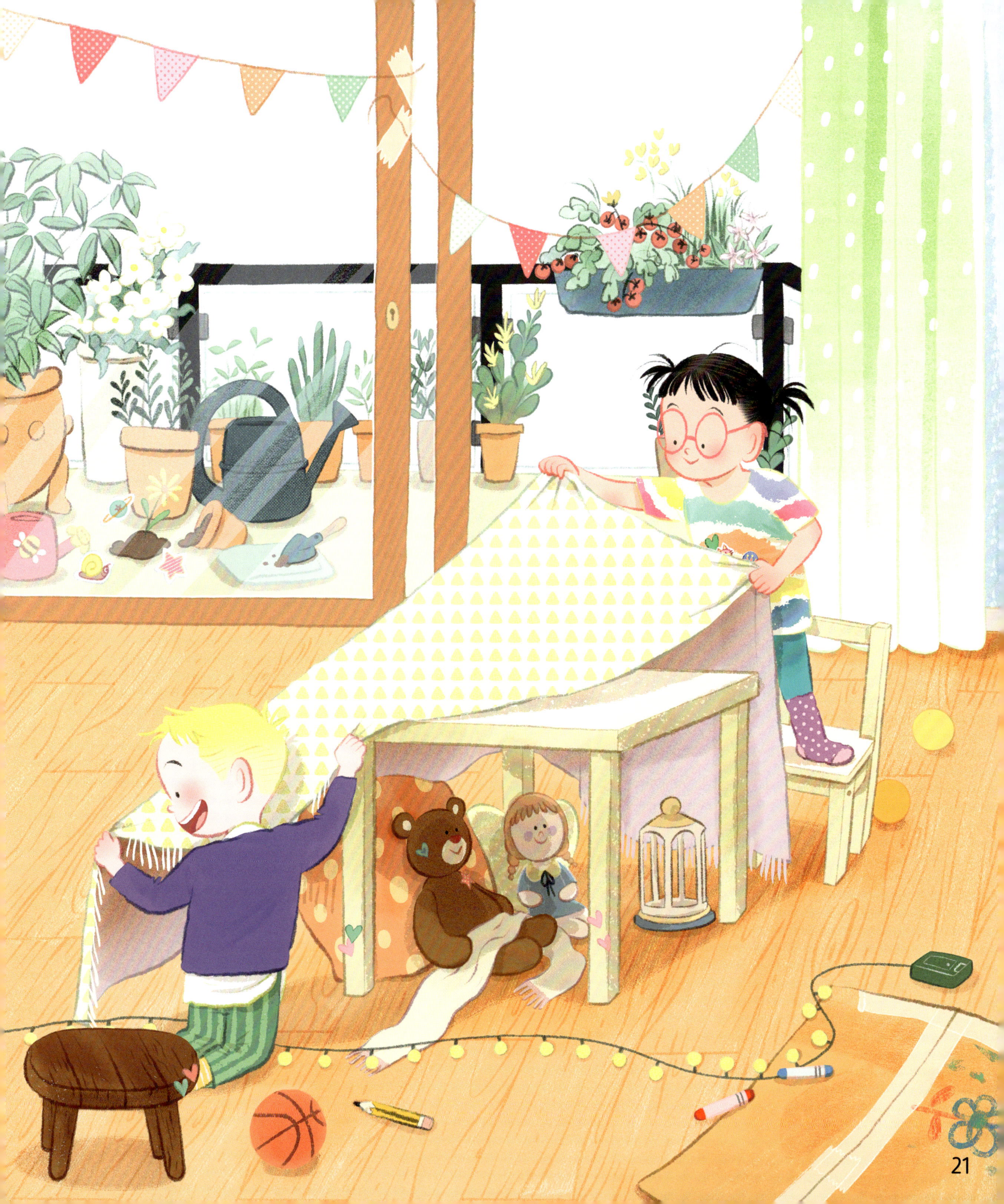

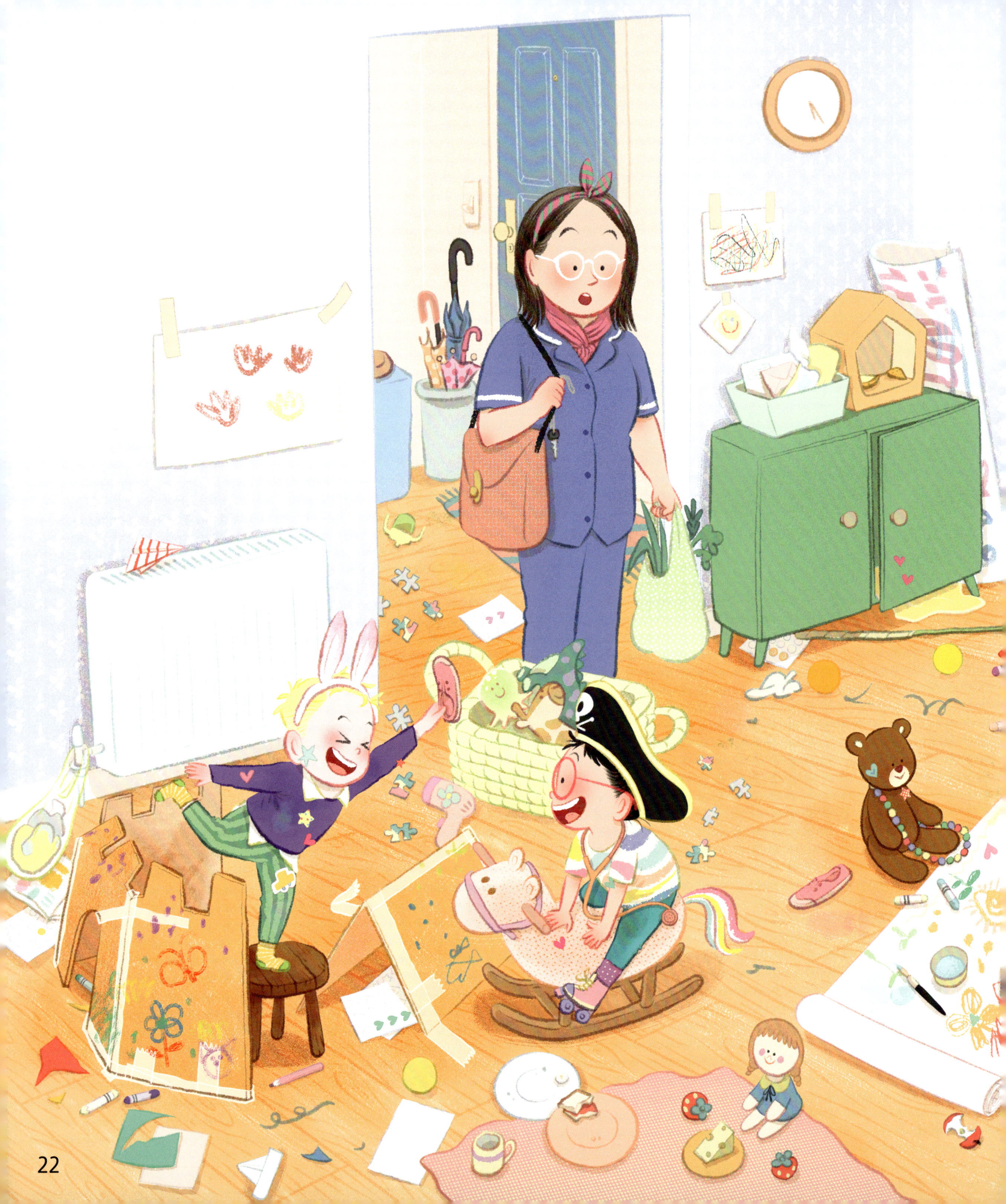

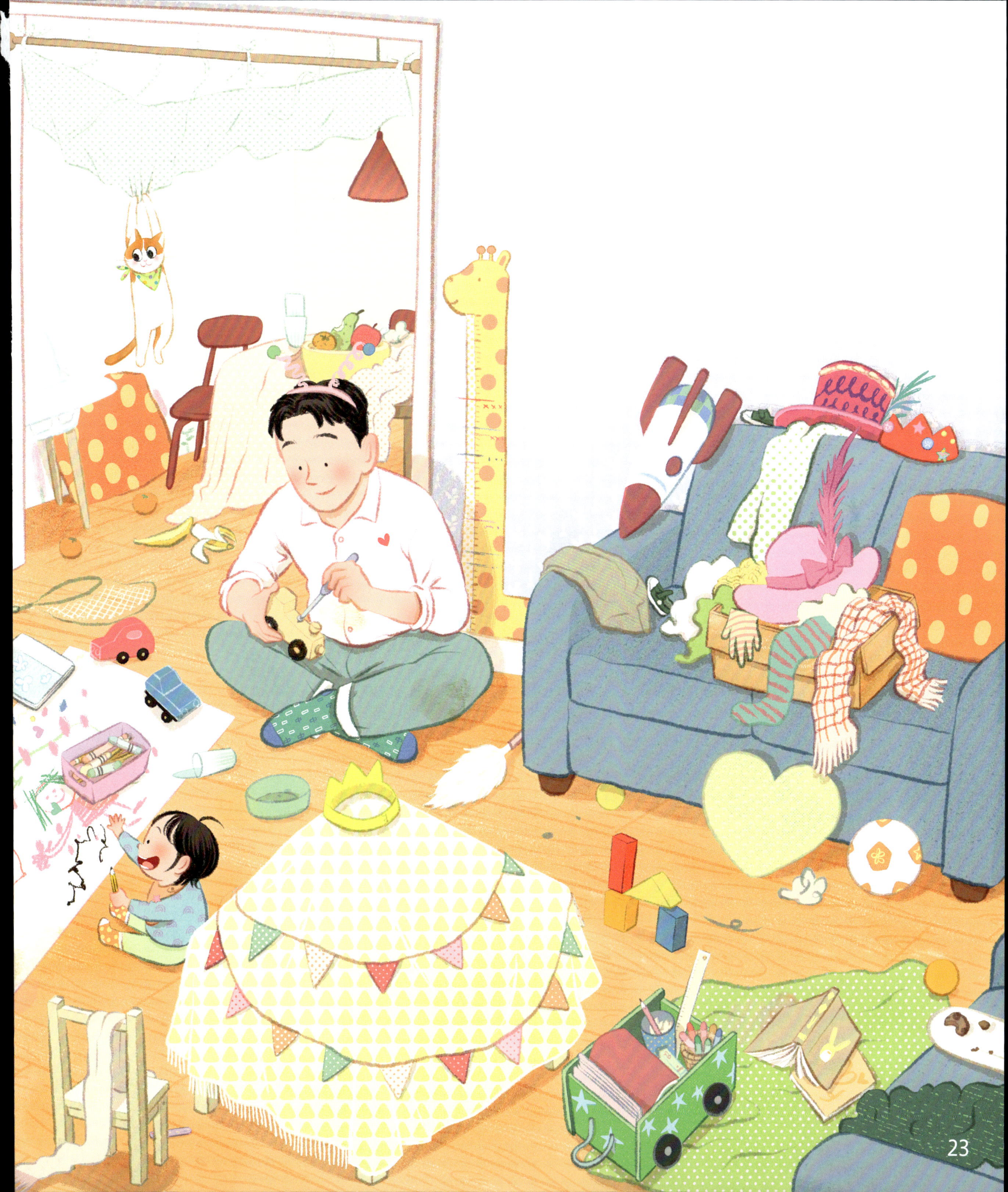

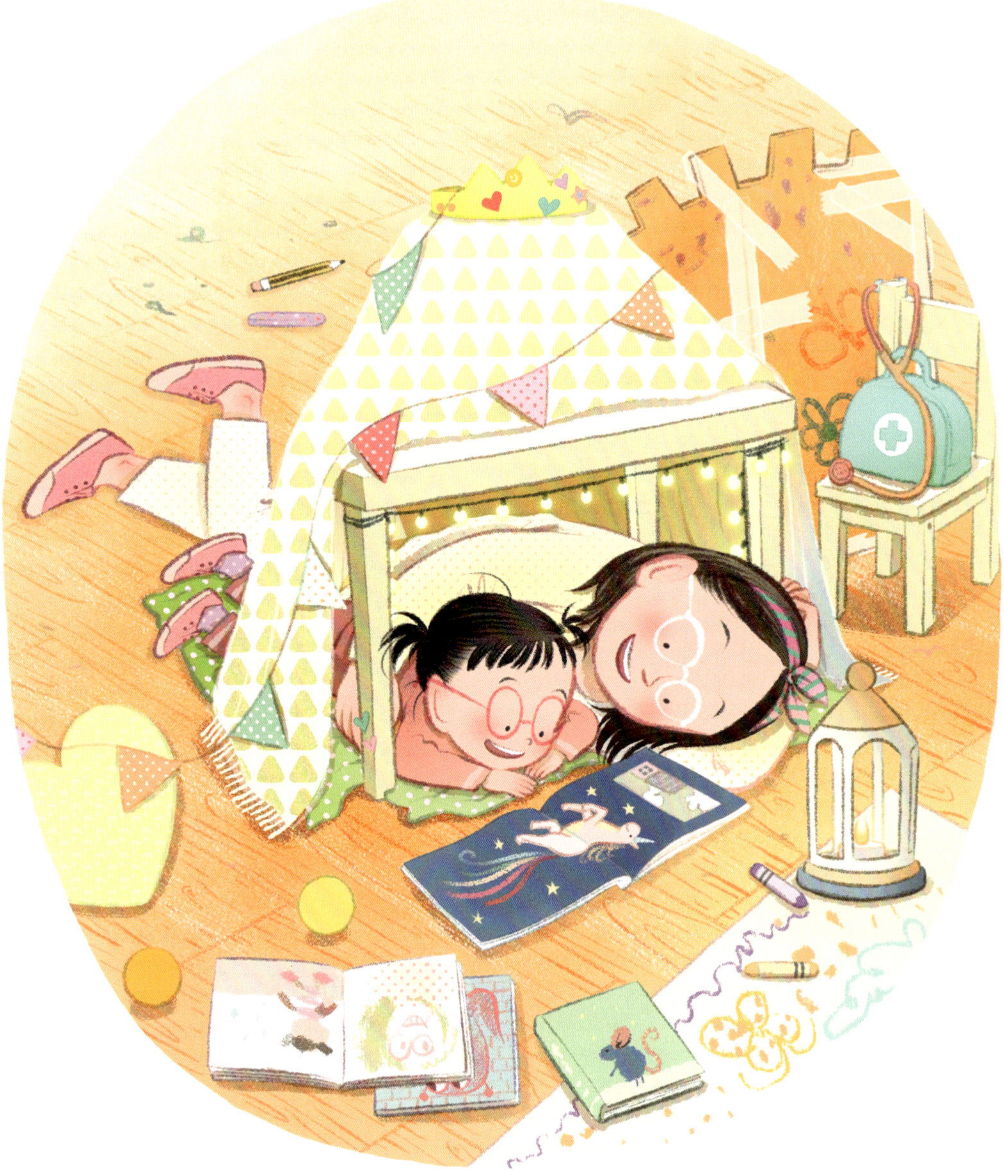